Jeff Zinn

About the Author

HOWARD ZINN—a historian, playwright, and social activist—was a shipyard worker and Air Force bombardier before he went to college under the GI Bill and received his Ph.D. from Columbia University. He has taught at Spelman College and Boston University, and has been a visiting professor at the University of Paris and the University of Bologna. He has received the Thomas Merton Award, the Eugene V. Debs Award, the Upton Sinclair Award, and the Lannan Literary Award. He lives in Massachusetts.

Other Books by Howard Zinn

La Guardia in Congress

The Southern Mystique

SNCC: The New Abolitionists

New Deal Thought (editor)

Vietnam: The Logic of Withdrawal

Disobedience and Democracy

The Politics of History

The Pentagon Papers: Critical Essays
(editor, with Noam Chomsky)

Postwar America

Justice in Everyday Life (editor)

A People's History of the United States

The Twentieth Century

Failure to Quit: Reflections of an Optimistic Historian

You Can't Be Neutral on a Moving Train

The Zinn Reader

The Future of History

Marx in Soho: A Play on History

On War

On History

Terrorism and War

Emma: A Play

Passionate Declarations

The
People
Speak

American Voices, Some Famous,

Some Little Known

Dramatic Readings Celebrating
the Enduring Spirit of Dissent

Edited by Howard Zinn

 Perennial

An Imprint of HarperCollins*Publishers*

FIRST EDITION

Designed by Nancy Singer Olaguera

Library of Congress Cataloging-in-Publication Data

Zinn, Howard.
    The people speak : American voices, some famous, some
little known / Howard Zinn.
        p. cm.
    ISBN 0-06-057826-2
    1. United States—History—Sources. 2. United States—
History—Anecdotes. 3. United States—Biography—Anecdotes.
I. Title.

E173.Z56 2004
973—dc21

                                                    2003056383

    10 11 12   ❖/RRD 10 9 8 7 6 5 4

To those Americans, past and present,
who knew what America could be

Contents

CONTENTS

Publisher's Note

In February of 2003 a remarkable event took place in New York City, a celebration of the millionth copy sold of Howard Zinn's *People's History of the United States*. In his opening remarks that evening, HarperCollins editor Hugh Van Dusen noted that in addition to having sold a million copies, Zinn's book has sold more copies every year than the year before through its twenty-three years.

For that evening, Zinn drew from his book, and from a few other sources, the statements of Americans—some famous, some little known—across the range of American history. These were read by a distinguished cast of actors and writers assembled for just that event: James Earl Jones, Alice Walker, Kurt Vonnegut, Alfre Woodard, Marisa Tomei, Danny Glover, Myla Pitt, Andre Gregory, Harris Yulin, Jeff Zinn.

They read the words of Christopher Columbus, a Lowell mill girl, Frederick Douglass, John Brown, Mark Twain, Helen Keller, Eugene Debs, a House Un-American Activities interrogation, Malcolm X, a Gulf War resister, a family member of a victim of the September 11 Twin Towers attack, and others.

The enthusiastic response to that evening at the 92nd Street Y led to the idea that theater companies, as well as high schools and colleges, might want to do their own readings of this highly charged material. HarperCollins agreed to undertake the publication.

The
People
Speak

1 | Introductory Excerpt from A People's History of the United States

NARRATOR

My viewpoint, in telling the history of the United States, is that we must not accept the memory of states as our own. Nations are not communities and never have been. The history of any country, presented as the history of a family, conceals fierce conflicts of interest. And in such a world of conflict, a world of victims and executioners, it is the job of thinking people, as Albert Camus suggested, not to be on the side of the executioners.

Thus, in that inevitable taking of sides which comes from selection and emphasis in history, I prefer to try to tell the story of the discovery of America from the viewpoint of the Arawaks, of the Constitution from the standpoint of the slaves, of the rise of industrialism as seen by the young women in the Lowell textile mills, the conquest of the Philippines as seen by black soldiers on Luzon, the postwar American empire as seen by peons in Latin America. And so on, to the limited extent that any one person, however he or she strains, can "see" history from the standpoint of others.

My point is not to grieve for the victims and denounce the executioners. Those tears, that anger, cast into the past, deplete our moral energy for the present. And the lines are not always clear. In the long run, the oppressor is also a victim. In the short run, the victims, themselves desperate and tainted with the culture that oppresses them, turn on other victims.

Still, understanding the complexities, I will be skeptical of governments and their attempts, through politics and culture, to ensnare ordinary people in a giant web of nationhood pretending to a common interest. I will try not to overlook the cruelties that victims inflict on one another as they are jammed together in the boxcars of the system. I don't want to romanticize them. But I do remember (in rough paraphrase) a statement I once read: "The cry of the poor is not always just, but if you don't listen to it, you will never know what justice is."

2 | Columbus and Las Casas

NARRATOR

*Arawak men and women, naked, tawny, and full of wonder,
emerged from their villages onto the island's beaches and swam
out to get a closer look at the strange big boat. When Columbus
and his sailors came ashore, carrying swords, speaking oddly,
the Arawaks ran to greet them, brought them food, water, gifts.*

He later wrote of this in his log.

COLUMBUS

They . . . brought us parrots and balls of cotton and spears and
many other things, which they exchanged for the glass beads
and hawks' bells. They willingly traded everything they
owned. . . . They were well-built, with good bodies and hand-
some features. . . . They do not bear arms, and do not know
them, for I showed them a sword, they took it by the edge and
cut themselves out of ignorance. They have no iron. Their
spears are made of cane. . . . They would make fine servants. . . .
With fifty men we could subjugate them all and make them do
whatever we want.

NARRATOR

We have no Indian voices to speak for the men and women of Hispaniola, but we have the volumes written by the Spanish priest Bartolomé de las Casas, who was an eyewitness to what happened after Columbus came.

LAS CASAS

These people are by nature the most humble, patient, and peaceable, holding no grudges, free from embroilments, neither excitable nor quarrelsome. These people are the most devoid of rancors, hatred or desire for vengeance of any people in the world. . . .

Yet into this sheepfold . . . there came some Spaniards, who immediately behaved like ravening wild beasts, wolves, tigers, or lions that had been starved for many days. And Spaniards have behaved in no other way during the past forty years, down to the present time, for they are still acting like ravening beasts, killing, terrorizing, afflicting, torturing, and destroying the native peoples, doing all of this with the strangest and most varied new methods of cruelty, never seen or heard of before, and to such a degree that this Island of Hispaniola, once so populous (having a population that I estimated to be more than three millions) has now a population of barely two hundred persons.

3 | *Shays' Rebellion*

NARRATOR

The American Revolution was not, as the orthodox histories would have it, the revolt of a unified people against England. The colonies were torn by class conflict—food riots and flour riots, and farmers' rebellions—in the hundred years before the Revolution. During the Revolutionary War, conflict emerged again, when ordinary soldiers, angered by their humiliating treatment and the special privileges of the officers, mutinied against George Washington. He ordered that some of them be executed by their fellow mutineers. After the war, veterans who had been given small amounts of land found themselves so heavily taxed they could not meet their payments. In western Massachusetts, thousands of farmers surrounded the courthouses where their farms were being auctioned off and refused to allow the courts to proceed. Eventually Shays' Rebellion, as it was called, was crushed, but it put a scare into the Founding Fathers, and when they met in 1787, shortly after, to create a Constitution, they made sure to set up a

government strong enough to put down rebellion. These are the
words of one of the participants in Shays' Rebellion, a man
named Plough Jogger.

PLOUGH JOGGER

I've labored hard all my days and fared hard. I have been greatly abused, have been obliged to do more than my part in the war; been loaded with class rates, town rates, province rates, Continental rates, and all rates . . . been pulled and hauled by sheriffs, constables and collectors, and had my cattle sold for less than they were worth.

I have been obliged to pay and nobody will pay me. I have lost a great deal by this man and that man and t'other man, and the great men are going to get all we have, and I think it is time for us to rise and put a stop to it, and have no more courts, nor sheriffs, nor collectors, nor lawyers, and I know that we are the biggest party, let them say what they will. We've come to relieve the distresses of the people. There will be no court until they have redress of their grievances.

4 | *Lowell Mill Girl*

NARRATOR

What is too often overlooked in the triumphal story of the growth of American industry in the nineteenth century is the human cost of that triumph: the lives cut short, the maimed bodies of the men and women who worked in the factories, the mills. In the Lowell, Massachusetts, textile mills of 1836, where girls went to work at the age of twelve and often died by the time they were twenty-five, one of the first strikes of mill girls took place. It is described by one of them, Harriet Hanson.

HARRIET HANSON

When it was announced that wages were to be cut down, great indignation was felt, and it was decided to strike, en masse. This was done. The mills were shut down, and the girls went in procession from their several corporations to the "grove" on Chapel Hill, and listened to "incendiary" speeches. . . .

One of the girls stood on a pump, and gave vent to the

feelings of her companions in a neat speech, declaring that it was their duty to resist all attempts at cutting down the wages. This was the first time a woman had spoken in public in Lowell, and the event caused surprise and consternation among her audience. . . .

My own recollection of this first strike (or "turn out" as it was called) is very vivid. I worked in a lower room, where I had heard the proposed strike fully, if not vehemently, discussed; I had been an ardent listener to what was said against this attempt at "oppression" on the part of the corporation, and naturally I took sides with the strikers. When the day came on which the girls were to turn out, those in the upper rooms started first, and so many of them left that our mill was at once shut down. Then, when the girls in my room stood irresolute, uncertain what to do, asking each other "Would you?" or "Shall we turn out?" and not one of them having the courage to lead off, I, who began to think they would not go out, after all their talk, became impatient, and started on ahead, saying, with childish bravado, "I don't care what you do, I am going to turn out, whether any one else does or not" and I marched out, and was followed by the others.

As I looked back at the long line that followed me, I was more proud than I have ever been at any success I may have achieved. . . .

5 | *Indian Removal*

NARRATOR

As part of the long process of driving the Indians off their native lands, Andrew Jackson in the 1830s signed an order to remove by force the Five Civilized Tribes from their territory in Florida, Georgia, and Alabama, and drive them westward across the Mississippi. There followed what became known as The Trail of Tears, in which sixteen thousand men, women, and children, surrounded by the United States Army, made the long trip westward, and four thousand of them died. The Cherokees and Seminoles had resisted, and spoke to the government of the United States.

THE CHEROKEES

We are aware that some persons suppose it will be for our advantage to remove beyond the Mississippi. We think otherwise. Our people universally think otherwise. . . . We wish to remain on the land of our fathers. We have a perfect and original right to remain without interruption or molestation. The treaties with us, and laws of the United States made in pursuance of treaties, guarantee our residence and our privileges, and secure us against intruders. Our only request is, that these treaties may be fulfilled, and these laws executed.

We entreat those to whom the foregoing paragraphs are addressed, to remember the great law of love: "Do to others as ye would that others would do to you." We pray them to remember that, for the sake of principle, their forefathers were compelled to leave, therefore driven from the old world, and that the winds of persecution wafted them over the great waters and landed them on the shores of the new world, when the Indian was the sole lord and proprietor of these extensive domains. Let them remember in what way they were received by the savage of America, when power was in his hand. . . .

We were all made by the same Great Father, and are all alike His Children. We all come from the same Mother, and were suckled at the same breast. Therefore we are brothers, and as brothers, should treat together in an amicable way.

THE SEMINOLES

Your talk is a good one, but my people cannot say they will go. We are not willing to do so. If suddenly we tear our hearts from the homes around which they are twined, our heartstrings will snap.

6 | *Women's Declaration of Rights*

NARRATOR

Women, black and white, played a critical part in the building of the antislavery movement in the United States. They worked in antislavery societies all over the country, gathering thousands of petitions to Congress. But when, in 1840, a World Anti-Slavery Society Convention met in London, there was a fierce argument about whether women could attend. The final vote was that they could only attend meetings in a curtained enclosure. They sat in silent protest in the gallery, and when they returned to the United States they began to lay the basis for the first Women's Rights Convention in history. It was held at Seneca Falls, New York, where Elizabeth Cady Stanton lived as a mother, a housewife, full of resentment at her condition, declaring: "A woman is a nobody. A wife is everything." The convention was attended by three hundred women and some men, who adopted a Declaration of Principles, making use of the language and rhythm of the Declaration of Independence.

DECLARATION OF SENTIMENTS
AND RESOLUTIONS

We hold these truths to be self-evident: that all men and women are created equal; that they are endowed by their Creator with certain inalienable rights; that among these are life, liberty, and the pursuit of happiness; that to secure these rights governments are instituted, deriving their just powers from the consent of the governed. Whenever any form of government becomes destructive of these ends, it is the right of those who suffer from it to refuse allegiance to it, and to insist upon the institution of a new government, laying its foundation on such principles, and organizing its powers in such form, as to them shall seem most likely to effect their safety and happiness. . . .

When a long train of abuses and usurpations, pursuing invariably the same object, evinces a design to reduce them under absolute despotism, it is their duty to throw off such government, and to provide new guards for their future security. Such has been the patient sufferance of the women under this government, and such is now the necessity which constrains them to demand the equal station to which they are entitled. . . .

Man has endeavored, in every way that he could, to destroy her confidence in her own powers, to lessen her self-respect, and to make her willing to lead a dependent and abject life. Now, in view of this entire disfranchisement of one-half the people of this country—their social and religious degradation—in view of the unjust laws above mentioned, and because women do feel themselves aggrieved, oppressed, and fraudulently deprived of their most sacred rights, we insist that they have immediate admission to all the rights and privileges which belong to them as citizens of the United States.

7 | *Frederick Douglass*

NARRATOR

Frederick Douglass, once a slave, became the brilliant and powerful leader of the antislavery movement. In 1852 he was asked to speak in celebration of the Fourth of July.

FREDERICK DOUGLASS

Fellow Citizens: Pardon me, allow me to ask, why am I called upon to speak here today? What have I, or those I represent, to do with your national independence? Are the great principles of political freedom and of natural justice, embodied in that Declaration of Independence, extended to us? And am I, therefore, called upon to bring our humble offering to the national altar, and to confess the benefits and express devout gratitude for the blessings resulting from your independence to us?

I am not included within the pale of this glorious anniversary! Your high independence only reveals the immeasurable distance between us. The blessings in which you, this day, rejoice, are not enjoyed in common. The rich inheritance of justice, liberty, prosperity and independence, bequeathed by your fathers, is shared by you, not by me. The sunlight that brought life and healing to you, has brought stripes and death to me. This Fourth of July is yours, not mine. You may rejoice. I must mourn. To drag a man in fetters into the grand illuminated temple of liberty, and call upon him to join you in joyous anthems, were inhuman mockery and sacrilegious irony. Do you mean, citizens, to mock me, by asking me to speak today?

Fellow citizens, above your national, tumultuous joy, I hear the mournful wail of millions! Whose chains heavy and grievous yesterday, are, today, rendered more intolerable by the jubilee shouts that reach them.

At a time like this, scorching irony, not convincing argument is needed. O! had I the ability, and could I reach the nation's ear, I would, today, pour out a fiery stream of biting ridicule, blasting reproach, withering sarcasm, and stern rebuke. For it is not light that is needed, but fire; it is not the gentle shower, but thunder. We need the storm, the whirlwind, the earthquake. The feeling of the nation must be quickened; the conscience of the nation must be roused; the propriety of the nation must be startled; the hypocrisy of the nation must be exposed, and its crimes against God and man must be proclaimed and denounced.

8 | *John Brown and Frederick Douglass*

NARRATOR

John Brown, more than any other white American, devoted his life, and finally sacrificed it, on behalf of freedom for the slave. His plan, impossible and courageous, was to seize the arsenal at Harpers Ferry, Virginia, with a band of black and white abolitionists, and set off a revolt of slaves throughout the South. The plan failed. Some of his men, including his son, were killed. John Brown was wounded, captured, and sentenced to death by hanging, with the state of Virginia and the government of the United States joining in his execution. When he was put to death, Ralph Waldo Emerson said: "He will make the gallows holy as the cross." Here John Brown addresses the court that ordered his hanging.

JOHN BROWN

Had I interfered in the manner, which I admit, had I so interfered in behalf of the rich, the powerful, the intelligent, the so-called great, or in behalf of any of their friends . . . or father, mother, brother, sister, wife or children, or any of that class, and suffered and sacrificed what I have in this interference, it would have been all right. Every man in this court would have deemed it an act worthy of reward rather than punishment.

This court acknowledges too, as I suppose, the validity of the law of God. I see a book kissed which I suppose to be the Bible, or at least the New Testament, which teaches me that all things whatsoever I would that men should do to me, I should do even so to them. I endeavored to act up to that instruction. . . . I believe that to have interfered as I have done, as I always have freely admitted, I have done, in behalf of His despised poor. I did not wrong, but right. Now if it is deemed necessary that I should forfeit my life for the furtherance of the ends of justice, and mingle my blood further with the blood of my children and with the blood of millions in this slave country whose rights are disregarded by wicked, cruel and unjust enactments, I submit. So let it be done.

NARRATOR
Twenty-two years later, in 1881, Frederick Douglass was asked to speak at a college in Harpers Ferry.

FREDERICK DOUGLASS
If John Brown did not end the war that ended slavery, he did at least begin the war that ended slavery. If we look over the

dates, places, and men, for which this honor is claimed, we shall find that not Carolina, but Virginia—not Fort Sumter, but Harpers Ferry and the arsenal—not Colonel Anderson, but John Brown began the war that ended American slavery and made this a free Republic. Until this blow was struck, the prospect for freedom was dim, shadowy, and uncertain. The irrepressible conflict was one of words, votes, and compromises. When John Brown stretched forth his arm, the sky was cleared. . . .

9 | *Henry Turner*

NARRATOR

After the Civil War, with the federal government enforcing the Fourteenth and Fifteenth Amendments to the Constitution, guaranteeing the right to vote to black people, African Americans were elected to governing bodies throughout the South. But after a few years of what might be called "Radical Reconstruction," the political and business interests of the North made a deal with those of the South, to withdraw federal power and allow the white South to have its way. Henry McNeal Turner, elected to the state legislature of Georgia, was expelled by that body in 1872, but before he left, he addressed his colleagues.

HENRY TURNER

Mr. Speaker. I wish the members of this House to understand the position that I take. I hold that I am a member of this body. Therefore, sir, I shall neither fawn or cringe before any party, nor stoop to beg them for my rights. I am here to demand my rights, and to hurl thunderbolts at the men who would dare to cross the threshold of my manhood.

The scene presented in this House, today, is one unparalleled in the history of the world. Never, in the history of the world, has a man been arraigned before a body clothed with legislative, judicial or executive functions, charged with the offense of being of a darker hue than his fellowmen. It has remained for the State of Georgia, in the very heart of the nineteenth century, to call a man before the bar, and there charge him with an act for which he is no more responsible than for the head which he carries upon his shoulders. The Anglo-Saxon race, sir, is a most surprising one. I was not aware that there was in the character of that race so much cowardice, or so much pusillanimity. I tell you, sir, that this is a question which will not die today. This event shall be remembered by posterity for ages yet to come, and while the sun shall continue to climb the hills of heaven.

We are told that if black men want to speak, they must speak through white trumpets; if black men want their sentiments expressed, they must be adulterated and sent through white messengers, who will quibble, and equivocate, and evade, as rapidly as the pendulum of a clock.

The great question, sir is this: Am I a man? If I am such, I claim the rights of a man.

Why, sir, though we are not white, we have accomplished much. . . . We have built up your country; we have worked in your fields, and garnered your harvests, for two hundred and fifty years! And what do we ask of you in return? Do we ask you for compensation for the sweat our fathers bore for you— for the tears you have caused, and the hearts you have broken, and the lives you have curtailed, and the blood you have spilled? Do we ask retaliation? We ask it not. We are willing to let the dead past bury its dead; but we ask you now for our RIGHTS.

10 | Mark Twain

NARRATOR

*The orthodox texts in American history pay much attention to
what was called "a splendid little war," the victory of the United
States in the three-month-long Spanish-American War of 1898.
But they slide quickly over the bloody conquest of the Philippines
that went on for years, which President McKinley said was
necessary to "civilize and Christianize" the Filipinos, and
Theodore Roosevelt hailed the Philippines as the newest outpost
of the American Empire. Roosevelt loved war and militarism
and when the army massacred six hundred Moros on a southern
island in the Philippines in 1906, Roosevelt congratulated the
commanding general. Here is Mark Twain's response.*

MARK TWAIN

This incident burst upon the world last Friday in an official
cablegram from the commander of our forces in the Philip-
pines to our Government at Washington. The substance of it
was as follows: A tribe of Moros, dark-skinned savages, had

fortified themselves in the bowl of an extinct crater not many miles from Jolo; and as they were hostiles, and bitter against us because we have been trying for eight years to take their liberties away from them, their presence in that position was a menace. Our commander, General Leonard Wood, ordered a reconnaissance. It was found that the Moros numbered six hundred, counting women and children; that their crater bowl was in the summit of a peak or mountain twenty-two hundred feet above sea level, and very difficult of access for Christian troops and artillery. Then General Wood ordered a surprise, and went along himself to see the order carried out.

General Wood's order was, "Kill or capture the six hundred."

There, with six hundred engaged on each side, we lost fifteen men killed outright, and we had thirty-two wounded—counting that nose and that elbow. The enemy numbered six hundred—including women and children—and we abolished them utterly, leaving not even a baby alive to cry for its dead mother. *This is incomparably the greatest victory that was ever achieved by the Christian soldiers of the United States.*

So far as I can find out, there was only one person among our eighty millions who allowed himself the privilege of a public remark on this great occasion—that was the President of the United States. All day Friday he was as studiously silent as the rest. But on Saturday he recognized that his duty required him to say something, and he took his pen and performed that duty. This is what he said:

Washington, March 10. Wood, Manila: I congratulate you and the officers and men of your command upon the brilliant feat of arms wherein you and they so well upheld the honor of the American flag. (Signed) Theodore Roosevelt.

I have read carefully the Treaty of Paris, and I have seen that we do not intend to free, but to subjugate the people of the Philippines. We have gone there to conquer, not to redeem. . . . It should, it seems to me, be our pleasure and duty to make those people free, and let them deal with their own domestic questions in their own way. And so I am an anti-imperialist. I am opposed to having the eagle put its talons on any other land.

11 | IWW and Lawrence Strike

NARRATOR

The IWW, Industrial Workers of the World, was a radical labor organization of the early twentieth century. It organized all workers—black, white, men, women, native-born, foreign, skilled, unskilled—which the American Federation of Labor refused to do. Its goal was revolutionary: to take over the industrial system and run it for the benefit of the people. When immigrant women in the textile mills in Lawrence, Massachusetts, went on strike in 1912, they were met with police violence and judicial intimidation. An IWW organizer, the poet Arturo Giovanitti, was arrested on spurious charges for murder. Here is his speech to the jury.

ARTURO GIOVANITTI

Mr. Foreman and Gentlemen of the Jury:

It is the first time in my life that I speak publicly in your wonderful language, and it is the most solemn moment in my life.

There has been brought only one side of this great industrial question, only the method and only the tactics. But what about the ethical part of this question? What about the better and nobler humanity where there shall be no more slaves, where no man will ever be obliged to go on strike in order to obtain fifty cents a week more, where children will not have to starve any more, where women no more will have to go and prostitute themselves, where at last there will not be any more slaves, any more masters . . . but just one great family of friends and brothers?

They say you are free in this great and wonderful country. I say that politically you are, and my best compliments and congratulations. But I say you cannot be half free and half slave, and economically all the working class in the United States are as much slaves now as the Negroes were forty and fifty years ago, because the man that owns the tool where another man works, the man that owns the house where this man lives, the man that owns the factory where this man wants to go to work—that man owns and controls the bread that that man eats and therefore owns and controls his mind, his body, his heart, and his soul. . . .

I am twenty-nine years old—not quite. I have a woman that loves me and that I love. I have a mother and father that are waiting for me. I have an ideal that is dearer to me than can be expressed or understood. And life has so many allurements and it is so nice and so bright and so wonderful that I felt the passion of living in my heart and I do want to live.

Whichever way you judge, gentlemen of the jury, I thank you.

12 | Mother Jones

NARRATOR

In the year 1914, a thousand miners, with wives and children, who had gone on strike against the Rockefeller-owned coal mines in southern Colorado, were holding out in a tent colony near the tiny hamlet of Ludlow. One day in April, the National Guard, financed by Rockefeller, began pouring machine-gun fire into the tent colony, and then came down from the hills and set fire to the tents. The next day the bodies of eleven children and two women were found, suffocated and burned to death. This became known as the Ludlow Massacre. Mother Mary Jones, an eighty-two-year-old organizer for the mine workers, had come to Colorado to support the miners, and on the eve of their strike, as they gathered in the Opera House in Trinidad, spoke to them.

MOTHER JONES

What would the coal in the mines be worth if you did not work to take it out?

The time is ripe for you to stand like men.

I know something about strikes. I didn't go into them yesterday.

I was carried eighty-four miles and landed in jail by a United States marshal in the night because I was talking to a miners' meeting. The next morning I was brought to court and the judge said to me, "Did you read my injunction? Did you understand that the injunction told you not to look at the miners?" "As long as the Judge who is higher than you leaves me sight, I will look at anything I want to," said I. The old judge died soon after that and the injunction died with him. At another time when in the courtroom the bailiff said to me, "When you are addressing the court you must say 'Your Honor.'" "I don't know whether he has any or not," said I.

Someone said to me, "You don't believe in charity work Mother." No I don't believe in charity; it is a vice. We need the upbuilding of justice to mankind; we don't need your charity, all we need is an opportunity to live like men and women in this country.

I want you to pledge yourselves in the convention to stand as one solid army against the foes of human labor. Think of the thousands who are killed every year and there is no redress for it. We will fight until the mines are made secure and human life valued more than props. Look things in the face. Don't fear a governor; don't fear anybody. You pay the governor, he has a right to protect you. You are the biggest part of the population in the state. You create its wealth, so I say let the fight go on; if nobody else will keep on, I will.

13 | Emma Goldman

NARRATOR

Emma Goldman, in the early part of the twentieth century, became one of the most powerful voices in America for anarchism, feminism, the rights of working people. She lectured all over the country on women's rights, on the theater of Shaw, Ibsen, Strindberg, on patriotism and war, and was arrested many times. She was jailed for opposing World War I and then was deported, under the personal supervision of J. Edgar Hoover. Here, in the year 1916, she addresses a courtroom where she has been charged with speaking about birth control.

EMMA GOLDMAN

Your Honor, I am charged with the crime of having given information to men and women as to how to prevent conception. For the last three weeks, every night before packed houses, a stirring social indictment is being played at the Candler Theater. I refer to "Justice" by John Galsworthy. The counsel for the Defense in summing up the charge against the defendant says among other things: "Your Honor: back of the commission of every crime, is life, palpitating life."

Now what is the palpitating life back of my crime? I will tell you, Your Honor. According to the bulletin of the Department of Health, 30,000,000 people in America are underfed.

Your Honor: what kind of children do you suppose these parents can bring into the world. I will tell you: children so poor and anemic that they take their leave from this, our kind world, before their first year of life. In that way, 300,000 babies, according to the baby welfare association, are sacrificed in the United States every year. This, Your Honor, is the palpitating life which has confronted me for many years, and which is back of the commission of my crime.

After all, the question of birth control is largely a workingman's question, above all a workingwoman's question. She it is who risks her health, her youth, her very life in giving out of herself the units of the race. She it is who ought to have the means and the knowledge to say how many children she shall give, and to what purpose she shall give them, and under what conditions she shall bring forth life.

And this is true, not only because of what I say or may not say; there is much profounder reason for the tremendous growth and importance of birth control. The reason is conditioned in the great modern social conflict, or rather social war, I should say. A war not for military conquest or material supremacy, a war of the oppressed and disinherited of the earth against their enemies, capitalism and the state, a war for a seat at the table of life, a war for well-being, for beauty, for liberty. Above all this war is for a free motherhood and a joyous, playful, glorious childhood.

14 | *Helen Keller*

NARRATOR

Helen Keller is presented to American schoolchildren as an extraordinary person who overcame blindness and deafness and became internationally famous. What our schools do not say about Helen Keller is that she was a socialist, a radical, that she opposed war and militarism, that she walked on picket lines. But she had to deal with charges that she was incompetent to judge such issues because of her disabilities. The editor of the Brooklyn Eagle, *who had once praised her lavishly, changed his mind when she declared herself a socialist. She wrote a letter to the newspaper in response, addressing it: "Poor blind* Eagle. . . ." *Here she speaks in Carnegie Hall, on the eve of America's entrance into World War I.*

HELEN KELLER

We are facing a grave crisis in our national life. The few who profit from the labor of the masses want to organize the work-ers into an army which will protect the interests of the capi-talists. You are urged to add to the heavy burdens you already bear the burden of a larger army and many additional warships. It is in your power to refuse. . . .

We are not preparing to defend our country—we have no enemies foolhardy enough to attempt to invade the United States.

Yet, everywhere, we hear fear advanced as argument for armament.

Congress is not preparing to defend the people of the United States. It is planning to protect the capital of American speculators and investors in Mexico, South America, China, and the Philippine Islands.

Every modern war has had its root in exploitation.

The preparedness propagandists have still another object, and a very important one. They want to give the people something to think about besides their own unhappy condition.

Every few days we are given a new war scare to lend realism to their propaganda.

They are taught that brave men die for their country's honor. What a price to pay for an abstraction—the lives of millions of young men; other millions crippled and blinded for life; existence made hideous for still more millions of human beings; the achievement and inheritance of generations swept away in a moment—and nobody better off for all the misery!

Strike against war, for without you no battles can be fought. Strike against manufacturing shrapnel and gas bombs and all other tools of murder. Strike against preparedness that means death and misery to millions of human beings. Be not dumb, obedient slaves in an army of destruction. Be heroes in an army of construction.

15 | *Eugene Debs*

NARRATOR

Eugene Debs led a national strike of railroad workers in 1894 and spent six months in jail for doing that. He went into prison a labor leader and came out a socialist. As leader of the Socialist Party he ran for president three times. When the United States entered World War I, President Wilson signed the Espionage Act, which provided long jail terms for anyone who said anything that might discourage recruitment in the armed forces. A filmmaker who made a movie about the American Revolution, depicting the British as enemies, was sentenced to ten years in prison, because now the British were our allies. His film was called The Spirit of '76 *and the court case against him was* U.S. vs. Spirit of '76.

Debs spoke against the war and was arrested for violating the Espionage Act; his conviction was upheld unanimously by the Supreme Court, which pointed to his statement that "the master class has always declared the wars, the subject class has always fought the battles." Here, at his trial in the fall of 1918, he is speaking to the court.

EUGENE DEBS

Your Honor, years ago I recognized my kinship with all living beings, and I made up my mind that I was not one bit better than the meanest on earth. I said then, and I say now, that while there is a lower class, I am in it, while there is a criminal element, I am of it, while there is a soul in prison, I am not free.

Your Honor, I have stated in this court that I am opposed to the social system in which we live; that I believe in a fundamental change—but if possible by peaceable and orderly means. . . .

Standing here this morning, I recall my boyhood. At fourteen I went to work in a railroad shop; at sixteen I was firing a freight engine on a railroad. I remember all the hardships and privations of that earlier day, and from that time until now my heart has been with the working class. I could have been in Congress long ago. I have preferred to go to prison. . . .

I am thinking this morning of the men in the mills and the factories; of the men in the mines and on the railroads. I am thinking of the women who for a paltry wage are compelled to work out their barren lives; of the little children who in this system are robbed of their childhood and in their tender years are seized in the remorseless grasp of Mammon and forced into the industrial dungeons, there to feed the monster machines while they themselves are being starved and stunted, body and soul. I see them dwarfed and diseased and their little lives broken and blasted because in this high noon of Christian civilization money is still so much more important than the flesh and blood of childhood. In very truth gold is god today and rules with pitiless sway in the affairs of men.

I am opposing a social order in which it is possible for one man who does absolutely nothing that is useful to amass a fortune of hundreds of millions of dollars, while millions of men and women who work all the days of their lives secure barely enough for a wretched existence.

This order of things cannot always endure. I have registered my protest against it. I recognize the feebleness of my effort, but, fortunately, I am not alone.

I can see the dawn of the better day for humanity. The people are awakening. In due time they will and must come to their own.

16 | The Harlem Renaissance

NARRATOR

The Harlem Renaissance is the name given to the burst of literary and artistic activity that took place in the 1920s and early 1930s. One of the poets of the Renaissance, Countee Cullen, wrote: "Yet do I marvel at this curious thing./To make a poet black and bid him sing."

Margaret Walker, James Weldon Johnson, Anne Spencer, and the extraordinary Zora Neale Hurston were part of that movement. One of its stars was Langston Hughes, whose social consciousness permeated his poetry. Here is his poem called "Ballad of the Landlord."

LANGSTON HUGHES

Landlord, landlord,
My roof has sprung a leak
Don't you 'member I told you about it
Way last week?

Landlord, landlord,
These steps is broken down.
When you come up yourself
It's a wonder you don't fall down.

Ten bucks you say I owe you?
Ten bucks you say is due?
Well, that's Ten Bucks more'n I'll pay you
Till you fix this house up new.

What? You gonna get eviction orders?
You gonna cut off my heat?
You gonna take my furniture an'
Throw it in the street?

Um-huh! You talking high and mighty.
Talk on—till you get through.
You isn't gonna be able to say a word
If I lay my fist on you.

Police! Police!
Come and get this man!
He's trying to ruin the government
And overturn the land!

Copper's whistle!
Patrol bell!
Arrest.

Precinct Station
Iron cell.
Headlines in press:

MAN THREATENS LANDLORD.

TENANT HELD. NO BAIL.

JUDGE GIVES NEGRO 90 DAYS IN COUNTY JAIL.

17 | Sit-Down Strike at Flint

NARRATOR

In the Depression years of the 1930s, workers in the great industries of America, in automobiles, rubber, steel, desperate to feed their families, rebelled against the powerful corporations that were dominating their lives. They formed unions, joined the Congress of Industrial Organizations, and, with or without the permission of their union leaders, went out on strike, facing police and armies and the National Guard. In 1936 they developed a new tactic, the sit-down strike. Instead of walking off the job, they stayed in the factories and created communities of resistance, defying their employers, the police, the courts. Women played a crucial part in those strikes. Here Genova Johnson Dollinger tells of the sit-down strike at the General Motors plant in Flint, Michigan.

GENOVA JOHNSON DOLLINGER

They used to say, "Once you pass the gates of General Motors, forget about the United States Constitution." Workers had no rights when they entered the plant. If a foreman didn't like the way you parted your hair—or whatever he didn't like about you . . . he could fire you. No recourse, not nothing.

After the first sit-down started, I went down to see what I could do to help. [T]hey said, "Go to the kitchen. We need a lot of help there." They didn't know what else to tell a woman to do. I said, "You've got a lot of little, skinny men around here who can't stand to be out on the cold picket lines for very long. They can peel potatoes as well as women can." Instead, I organized a children's picket line. The picture of my two-year-old son, Jarvis, holding a picket sign saying, "My daddy strikes for us little tykes," went all over the nation. The next day, we decided to organize the women. We thought that if women can be that effective in breaking a strike, they could be just as effective in helping to win it.

I thought, "The women can break this up." So, I appealed to the women in the crowd, "Break through those police lines." In the dusk, I could barely see one woman struggling to come forward. A cop had grabbed her by the back of her coat. She just pulled out of the coat and started walking down to the battle zone. As soon as that happened there were other women and men who followed. The police wouldn't shoot people in the back as they were coming down, so that was the end of the battle. When those spectators came into the center of the battle and the police retreated, there was a big roar of victory. That battle became known as the Battle of Bulls Run because we made the cops run.

We didn't know that nothing like that had ever been organized before, at least not in this country. We didn't know we were making history. We didn't have time to think about it.

After we sat down in Flint, which was the heart of the General Motors production empire, fifteen GM plants across the country went on strike. And the news went out about the role women could play. Following the strike, the auto worker became a different human being.

18 | Catch-22

NARRATOR

When Studs Terkel published his interviews with veterans of World War II, he put the title, The Good War, *in quotation marks. He was recognizing that in the perspective of history there were questions raised about the "good war," about Hiroshima and Nagasaki, about Dresden and Tokyo, about the indiscriminate bombing of civilian populations, about the ultimate value of any war, however noble the cause. War was always the killing of innocents—civilians and soldiers. And the military, however "good" the war, was always corrupt, and contained, in the best of situations, elements of fascism. In his novel* Catch-22, *Joseph Heller captured the absurdity and cruelty that pervades military life. In this passage, Yossarian's friend Clevinger is facing military justice.*

FROM CATCH-22

"Justice?" The colonel was astounded. "What is justice."
    "Justice, sir. . . ."

"That's not what justice is," the colonel jeered and began pounding the table again with his big fat hand. "That's what Karl Marx is. I'll tell you what justice is. Justice is a knee in the gut from the floor on the chin at night sneaky with a knife brought up down on the magazine of a battleship and sand-bagged underhanded in the dark without a word of warning. Garroting. That's what justice is when we've all got to be tough enough and rough enough to fight Billy Petrolle. From the hip. Get it? . . ."

Clevinger was guilty, of course, or he would not have been accused, and since the only way to prove it was to find him guilty, it was their patriotic duty to do so. . . .

It was all very confusing to Clevinger. There were many strange things taking place, but the strangest of all, to Clevinger, was the hatred, the brutal, uncloaked, inexorable hatred of the members of the Action Board. . . . They were three grown men and he was a boy, and they hated him and wished him dead. . . .

Yossarian had done his best to warn him the night before. "You haven't got a chance, kid," he had told him glumly. "They hate Jews."

"But I'm not Jewish," answered Clevinger.

"It will make no difference," Yossarian promised, and Yossarian was right. "They're after everybody."

Clevinger recoiled from their hatred as though from a blinding light. These three men who hated him spoke his language and wore his uniform, but he saw their loveless faces set immutably into cramped, mean lines of hostility and understood instantly that nowhere in the world, not in all the fascist tanks or planes or submarines . . . not even among all the expert gunners of the crack Hermann Goering Antiaircraft Division or among the grisly connivers in all the beer halls in Munich and everywhere else, were there men who hated him more.

19 | HUAC Interrogation

NARRATOR

The end of World War II brought no peace, but an arms race between the United States and the Soviet Union, and an intense fear of Communism pervading American society. Abroad it took the form of seeing every revolutionary movement as part of a world Communist conspiracy. At home there was a near-hysterical search for Communist influence everywhere, leading to loyalty oaths for government employees, secret FBI surveillance of hundreds of thousands of Americans, and congressional inquisitions into the political ideas and affiliations of educators and people in the arts. The House Committee on Un-American Activities decided there was Communist influence in the film industry. Informers named actors and directors as members of the Communist Party, and these were then called before the committee to inform on others, under penalty of prison if they did not cooperate, or of being blacklisted in their profession. Lionel Stander, a veteran Hollywood actor, dueled with the committee.

1953: HUAC Hearings

MR. STANDER: Does the Committee charge me with being a Communist?

MR. VELDE: Mr. Stander, will you let me tell you whether you are charged with being a Communist? Will you be quiet just for a minute while I will tell you what you are here for?

MR. STANDER: Yes, I would like to hear.

MR. VELDE: You are here to give us information which will enable us to do the work that was assigned to us by the House of Representatives, which is a duty imposed upon us to investigate reports regarding subversive activities in the United States.

MR. STANDER: Well, I am more than willing to cooperate—

MR. VELDE: Now, just a minute.

MR. STANDER: Because I have—I know of some subversive activities in the entertainment industry and elsewhere in the country.

MR. VELDE: Mr. Stander, the Committee is interested in any subversive knowledge you have.

MR. STANDER: I have knowledge of some subversive action . . . and I can help the Committee if it is really interested.

MR. VELDE: Mr. Stander—

MR. STANDER: I know of a group of fanatics who are desperately trying to undermine the Constitution of the United States by depriving artists and others of life, liberty, and pursuit of happiness without due process of law. If you are interested in that, I would like to tell you about it. I can tell names and I can cite instances, and I am one of the first victims of it, and if you are interested in that—and also a group of ex-Bundists, America Firsters, and anti-Semites, people who hate everybody, including Negroes, minority groups, and most likely themselves—

MR. VELDE: Now Mr. Stander—

MR. STANDER: And there are people engaged in the conspiracy, outside of all the legal processes to undermine our very fundamental American concepts upon which our entire system of jurisprudence exists—

MR. VELDE: Mr. Stander, unless you begin to answer these questions and act like a witness in a reasonable, dignified manner, under the rules of the Committee, I will be forced to have you removed from this room.

MR. STANDER: I am deeply shocked, Mr. Chairman.

20 | *Fannie Lou Hamer*

*In the summer of 1964, the black men and women of
Mississippi, joined by a thousand young volunteers from the
north, formed the Freedom Democratic Party in defiance of the
all-white Democratic Party of Mississippi. When the
Democratic National Convention met in Atlantic City, black
activists in the Freedom Democratic Party traveled by bus from
Mississippi to demand that the all-white delegates from
Mississippi (whose population was 40 percent black) be
replaced by a black and white delegation that would be
representative of the state. Fannie Lou Hamer, a sharecropper
who had become a leader of the movement in Mississippi, spoke
to the Credentials Committee, citing her own experience, about
what happened to black people in Mississippi who tried to vote.
Her eloquence on this occasion, which was nationally televised,
so worried President Lyndon Johnson that he issued a White
House announcement to interrupt her testimony. The
Democratic Party would not seat the black delegates, offering*

them instead two nonvoting seats, which they refused. Here is a portion of Mrs. Hamer's testimony.

FANNIE LOU HAMER

Mr. Chairman, and the Credentials Committee, my name is Mrs. Fannie Lou Hamer, and I live at 626 East Lafayette Street, Ruleville, Mississippi, Sunflower County, the home of Senator James O. Eastland, and Senator Stennis.

It was the 31st of August in 1962 that 18 of us traveled 26 miles to the county courthouse in Indianola to try to register to try to become first-class citizens. . . . The plantation owner came, and said. "Fannie Lou, if you don't go down and withdraw your registration, you will have to leave because we are not ready for that in Mississippi."

And I addressed him and told him and said, "I didn't try to register for you. I tried to register for myself."

I had to leave that same night.

And in June, the 9th, 1963, I had attended a voter registration workshop, was returning back to Mississippi. Ten of us was traveling by the Continental Trailway bus. When we got to Winona, Mississippi, "It was a State Highway Patrolman and a Chief of Police ordered us out."

Somebody screamed, "Get that one there," and when I went to get in the car, then the man told me I was under arrest, and he kicked me.

I was carried to the county jail, and I was placed in a cell with a young woman called Miss Ivesta Simpson. I began to hear the sounds and horrible screams, and I could hear somebody say, "Can you say, yes, sir, nigger? Can you say yes, sir?"

She would say, "Yes, I can say yes, sir."

"So, say it."

She says, "I don't know you well enough."

They beat her, I don't know how long, and after a while she began to pray, and asked God to have mercy on those people.

All of this is on account we want to register, to become first-class citizens, and if the Freedom Democratic Party is not seated now, I question America, is this America, the land of the free and the home of the brave where we have to sleep with our telephones off the hooks because our lives be threatened daily because we want to live as decent human beings in America.

Thank you.

21 | Malcolm X

In the struggle for racial equality, not all black people accepted Martin Luther King Jr.'s message of love and nonviolence. Soon after the 1963 March on Washington, in which King spoke of his "dream," four black girls were killed in the bombing of a Birmingham church. For Malcolm X, who grew up in a northern ghetto, spent time in prison, and became a Muslim, this pointed to the limitations of the civil rights movement. That fall, Malcolm X addressed a meeting in Detroit. Two years later he would be assassinated.

MALCOLM X

As long as the white man sent you to Korea you bled. He sent you to Germany, you bled. He sent you to the South Pacific to fight the Japanese, you bled. You bleed for white people, but when it comes to seeing your own churches being bombed and little black girls murdered, you haven't got any blood. You bleed when the white man says bleed; you bite when the white man says bite, and you bark when the white man says bark. I hate to say this about us, but it's true. How are you going to be nonviolent in Mississippi, as violent as you were in Korea? How can you justify being nonviolent in Mississippi and Alabama, when your churches are being bombed, and your little girls are being murdered?

If violence is wrong in America, violence is wrong abroad. If it is wrong to be violent defending black women and black children and black babies and black men, then it is wrong for America to draft us and make us violent abroad in defense of her. And if it is right for America to draft us, and teach us how to be violent in defense of her, then it is right for you and me to do whatever is necessary to defend our own people right here in this country.

Right at that time Birmingham had exploded. . . . That's when Kennedy sent in the troops, down in Birmingham. After that, Kennedy got on the television and said "this is a moral issue." That's when he said he was going to put out a civil rights bill. And when he mentioned civil rights bill and the Southern crackers started talking bout how they were going to boycott or filibuster it, then the Negroes started talking—about what? That they were going to march on Washington, march on the Senate, march on the White House, march on the Congress, and tie it up, bring it to a halt, not let the government proceed. They even said they were going out to the airport and lay down on the runway and not let any airplanes land. I'm telling you what they said. That was revolution. That was revolution. That was the black revolution.

It was the grass roots out there in the street. It scared the white man to death, scared the power structure in Washington, D.C., to death; I was there. When they found out that this black steamroller was going to come down on the capital they called in Wilkins, they called in Randolph, they called in these national Negro leaders that you respect and told them, "Call it off," Kennedy said. "Look you are letting this thing go too far." And Old Tom said, "Boss, I can't stop it because I didn't start it." I'm telling you what they said. They said, "I'm not even in it, much less at the head of it." They said, "These Negroes are doing things on their own."

22 | Vietnam

NARRATOR

In the great national campaign against the war in Vietnam, young black people in the southern civil rights movement were among the first protesters, among the first imprisoned for resisting the draft. On April 4, 1967, Martin Luther King Jr., against the advice of more conservative black leaders, addressed an audience at the Riverside Church in New York City and spoke out powerfully against the war.

MARTIN LUTHER KING JR.

I come to this magnificent house of worship tonight because my conscience leaves me no other choice. "A time comes when silence is betrayal." That time has come for us in relation to Vietnam.

In 1957, when a group of us formed the Southern Christian Leadership Conference, we chose as our motto: "To save the soul of America." In a way we were agreeing with Langston Hughes, that black bard of Harlem, who had written earlier:

O, yes, I say it plain,
America never was America to me,
And yet I swear this oath—
America will be!

Somehow this madness must cease. We must stop now. I speak as a child of God and brother to the suffering poor of Vietnam. I speak for those whose land is being laid waste, whose homes are being destroyed, whose culture is being subverted. I speak for the poor of America who are paying the double price of smashed hopes at home and death and corruption in Vietnam. I speak as a citizen of the world, for the world as it stands aghast at the path we have taken. I speak as one who loves America, to the leaders of our own nation: The great initiative in this war is ours; the initiative to stop it must be ours.

I am convinced that if we are to get on the right side of the world revolution, we as a nation must undergo a radical revolution of values. We must rapidly begin [applause], we must rapidly begin the shift from a thing-oriented society to a person-oriented society. When machines and computers, profit motives and property rights, are considered more important than people, the giant triplets of racism, extreme materialism, and militarism are incapable of being conquered.

A true revolution of values will soon look uneasily on the glaring contrast of poverty and wealth. The Western arrogance of feeling that it has everything to teach others and nothing to learn from them is not just.

A true revolution of values will lay hand on the world order and say of war, "This way of settling differences is not just." This business of burning human beings with napalm, of filling our nation's homes with orphans and widows, of injecting poisonous drugs of hate into the veins of peoples normally humane, of sending men home from dark and bloody battlefields physically handicapped and psychologically deranged, cannot be reconciled with wisdom, justice, and love. A nation that continues year after year to spend more money on military defense than on programs of social uplift is approaching spiritual death [sustained applause].

Now let us begin. Now let us rededicate ourselves to the long and bitter, but beautiful, struggle for a new world.

23 | The Women's Movement

The rebellious spirit of the 1960s showed itself not only in the civil rights movement and the antiwar movement but also in an unprecedented emergence of a movement for gay and lesbian rights, as well as in the exciting new movement for the rights of women. Too often, that movement spoke for white women, but here Abbey Lincoln, the jazz singer, speaks for women of color.

ABBEY LINCOLN

We are the women who were kidnapped and brought to this continent as slaves. We are the women who were raped, are still being raped, and our bastard children snatched from our breasts and scattered to the winds to be lynched, castrated, de-egoed, robbed, burned, and deceived.

We are the women whose strong and beautiful Black bodies were—and are—still being used as a cheap labor force for Miss Anne's kitchen and Mr. Charlie's bed, whose rich, black and warm milk nurtured—and still nurtures—the heir to the racist and evil slavemaster.

We are the women who dwell in the hell-hole ghettos all over the land. We are the women whose bodies are sacrificed, as living cadavers, to experimental surgery in the white man's hospitals for the sake of white medicine. We are the women who are invisible on the television and movie screens, on the Broadway stage. We are the women who are lusted after, sneered at, leered at, hissed at, yelled at, grabbed at, tracked down by white degenerates in our own pitiable, poverty-stricken, and prideless neighborhoods.

We are the women whose hair is compulsively fried, whose skin is bleached, whose nose is "too big," whose mouth is "too big and loud," "whose behind is "too big and broad," whose feet are "too big and flat," whose face is "too black and shiny," and whose suffering and patience are too long and enduring to be believed.

Who are just too damned much for everybody . . .

Who will revere the black woman? Who will keep our neighborhoods safe for Black innocent womanhood? Black womanhood is outraged and humiliated. Black womanhood cries for dignity and restitution and salvation. Black womanhood wants and needs protection, and keeping, and holding. Who will assuage her indignation? Who will keep her precious and pure? Who will glorify and proclaim her beautiful image? To whom will she cry rape?

24 | Chicanos and Vietnam

NARRATOR

The opposition of the Latino population in the United States to the war in Vietnam has been little noticed, even by the antiwar movement. But some of the largest demonstrations against the war were of Chicanas and Chicanos of the West Coast. At one point (according to the extraordinary collection Aztlán in Viet Nam) between 20,000 and 30,000 people gathered in Laguna Park in Los Angeles, in August of 1970, to protest the war. The Chicana poet María Herrera-Sobek expresses that strong feeling in two of her poems.

MARÍA HERRERA-SOBEK

UNTITLED

> We saw them coming
> in funeral black bags
> body bags they called them
> eyes locked forever
> they were our

brown men
shot
in a dishonest war
Vietnam taught us
not to trust
anyone over thirty
for *they* had the guns
and the power
to send our boyfriends
fathers, brothers
off to war
while they sauntered
in lily-white
segregated
country clubs
a bomb was planted
in our minds
a bomb exploded
in 1969
Watts, East Los Angeles
Black Panthers
Brown Berets
Drank the night
and lighted up the sky
with homemade
fireworks
the war had come
to roost

in our own backyard
made in the USA guns
turned inward
and shot our young
Dead in the streets
Dead in the battlefields
Dead in the schools
and yet a plaintive song
Crashing against the crackling explosion
of a Molotov cocktail
insisted
"We shall overcome."

VIETNAM: A FOUR-LETTER WORD

Vietnam
Was a four-letter word
The stench of napalm
In the air
Seared our nightmares
California palm trees
Waving fronds of anti-patriotism
"Hell no, we won't go"
Was not a TV jingle
It was the chant
Of those who marched
To a different tune

Of those who wore peace
On their foreheads
Love on their sleeves
And American flags
On their behinds

25 | Gulf War Resister

NARRATOR

Early in 1991, President George H. W. Bush sent American troops into Iraq, presumably to liberate Kuwait from the control of Saddam Hussein, more likely to assure American power in the oil-rich countries of the Middle East. The government had learned from the Vietnam experience that an antiwar movement must not be allowed time to develop, that U.S. casualties must be kept low, and that information about the war must be controlled. A massive air attack quickly defeated the forces of Saddam Hussein, and the American people were kept ignorant of the large numbers of casualties among Iraqi civilians. Nevertheless, a protest movement developed, and there were refusals among the military to participate in the war. A U.S. Navy Reserve corpsman named James Lawrence Harrington wrote a letter of resignation to his commander.

JAMES LAWRENCE HARRINGTON

There comes a time in life when maintaining silence is but a betrayal of one's own spiritual core of being. Such a time has come and I must declare from the expansion of my heart and over the limited sphere of my mind that I am a conscientious objector opposed to any and all wars. The power and command of my faith dictates that I work diligently and completely to stop war. To this end, do I dedicate the efforts of my life.

I do not hold that the absence of participation in war is itself a peace. Through the power of the people, peace is an active force that can and must spread to all nations, including our own. Our nation suffers from a deep malady in its consciousness that leads it down the path of continual violence and strife. I seek not only to stop this impending war in the Persian Gulf, but to also treat our own profound sickness.

War is but a symptom of a greater concern. I prescribe the treatment of a radical revolution within our nation from that of a "thing"-oriented society to a "person"-oriented community. We must learn to love and respect all people for the sake of divinity and basic goodness that dwells within them.

When we deny people the right to exist and to self-determination, we are assuring our own self-destruction. In order to save my nation and in order not to betray my own soul, I take this open stance of opposition to all wars.

Sincerely,
James Lawrence Harrington

26 | Poverty in Our Time

NARRATOR

The administration of Ronald Reagan began an attack on welfare, on aid to single mothers, on food stamps, on health care for the poor. That attack would culminate during the Clinton administration with the ending of federal guarantees to women with dependent children. In the early Reagan years, a mother wrote to a local newspaper, responding to the claim that government was not needed, that private enterprise, the so-called free market, would take care of poverty.

MOTHER

I am on Aid to Families with Dependent Children, and both my children are in school. . . . I have graduated from college with distinction, 128th in a class of over 1,000, with a B.A. in English and sociology. I have experience in library work, child care, social work and counseling. . . . I have applied for jobs paying as little as $8,000 a year. I work part-time in a library for $3.50 an hour, welfare reduces my allotment to compensate. . . .

It appears we have employment offices that can't employ, governments that can't govern and an economic system that can't produce jobs for people ready to work. . . .

Last week I sold my bed to pay for the insurance on my car, which in the absence of mass transportation I need to go job hunting. I sleep on a piece of rubber foam somebody gave me.

So this is the great American dream my parents came to this country for: Work hard, get a good education, follow the rules, and you will be rich. I don't want to be rich. I just want to be able to feed my children and live with some semblance of dignity. . . .

27 | Post–September 11: Families for Peaceful Tomorrows

NARRATOR

Immediately after the terrorist attacks on the Twin Towers and the Pentagon on September 11, 2001, President George W. Bush proclaimed a "war on terrorism" and soon after began the bombardment of Afghanistan. But some of the families who had lost loved ones in the attack refused to support what the government was doing and formed a group called Families for Peaceful Tomorrows. The family of Phyllis and Orlando Rodriguez, whose son Greg was among the many missing from the World Trade Center, wrote to the New York Times: *"We . . . sense that our government is heading in the direction of violent revenge. . . . It is not the way to go. It will not avenge our son's death. . . . Not in our son's name."*

A woman named Amber Amundson sent a statement to the Chicago Tribune.

AMBER AMUNDSON

My husband, Craig Scott Amundson, of the U.S. Army, lost his life in the line of duty at the Pentagon on September 11th, as the world looked on in horror and disbelief. . . .

Losing my 28-year-old husband and father of our two young children is a terrible and painful experience. . . .

I have heard angry rhetoric by some Americans, including many of our nation's leaders, who advise a heavy dose of revenge and punishment. To those leaders, I would like to make clear that my family and I take no comfort in your words of rage. If you choose to respond to this incomprehensible brutality by perpetuating violence against other innocent human beings, you may not do so in the name of justice for my husband. . . .

Craig would not have wanted a violent response to avenge his death. And I cannot see how good can come out of it. We cannot solve violence with violence. Mohandas Gandhi said: "An eye for an eye only makes the whole world blind."

I call on our national leaders to find the courage to respond to this incomprehensible tragedy by breaking the cycle of violence. I call on them to marshal this great nation's skills and resources to lead a worldwide dialogue on freedom from terror and hate.

Acknowledgments

Anthony Arnove and Joey Fox were of great help in finding material for these readings, some of which will appear in a Seven Stories Press book, *Voices from a People's History*. Leslie Cohen at HarperCollins, along with Susan Engel, Sidney Burgos, John Kelly, Gail Martin, and Deborah Seymour of the 92nd Street Y were essential in organizing the February 27, 2003, event where these readings took place. Harris Yulin, one of the actors participating, played a critical role in finding other actors and in staging the event. My editor at HarperCollins, Hugh Van Dusen, who introduced the evening, gave strong support throughout, as did David Semanki, also of HarperCollins.

Permissions

 Perennial

Books by Howard Zinn:

A PEOPLE'S HISTORY OF THE UNITED STATES: *1492–Present*
ISBN 0-06-052837-0 (paperback)

Newly revised and updated from its original landmark publication in 1980. Zinn throws out the official version of history taught in schools—with emphasis on great men in high places—to focus on the street, the home, and the workplace. This latest edition contains two new chapters that cover the Clinton presidency, the 2000 election, and the "War on Terrorism."

"Historians may well view it as a step toward a coherent new version of American history." —Eric Foner, *New York Times Book Review*

THE TWENTIETH CENTURY: *A People's History*
ISBN 0-06-053034-0 (paperback)

Designed for general readers and students of modern American history, this reissue of the twentieth-century chapters from Howard Zinn's popular *A People's History of the United States* is brought up-to-date with new chapters on Clinton's presidency, the 2000 election, and the "War on Terrorism."

"Professor Zinn writes with an enthusiasm rarely encountered in the leaden prose of academic history." —*New York Times Book Review*

PASSIONATE DECLARATIONS: *Essays on War and Justice*
ISBN 0-06-055767-2 (paperback)

A collection of passionate, honest, and piercing essays that focus on American political ideology. Complete with a new preface by the author.

"A shotgun blast of revisionism that aims to shatter all the comfortable myths of American political discourse." —*Los Angeles Times*

THE PEOPLE SPEAK: *American Voices, Some Famous, Some Little Known*
ISBN 0-06-057826-2 (paperback)

A wonderful selection of American voices from Columbus to the present, interwoven with commentary by Zinn. Including selections from a Lowell Mill worker, Frederick Douglass, Mark Twain, Helen Keller, Malcolm X, and a Gulf War resister.